MW01227456

Japanese Reading for JLPT N5

Master the Japanese Language
Proficiency Test N5

Clay & Yumi Boutwell

ISBN-13: 9781677888399

INTRODUCTION

Taking the Japanese Language Proficiency Test is a great way to not only assess your Japanese skills but also to give yourself a concrete goal for your studies.

Goals help increase motivation and motivation almost always results in progress. Also, by making plans to sit in a test in a different city (usually), you are making a major investment of time and money. There are few pressures in life that can motivate better than time or money. That's why I always recommend signing up and studying for the JLPT for any serious student of Japanese.

Still, this book should help beginners even if you are not planning to take the test. If you have learned hiragana and katakana, know a few dozen kanji, and can understand very basic Japanese grammar, this book is for you.

While we do include a few N4-level kanji (with furigana), the majority of the kanji shown is for N5. Vocabulary, likewise, is mostly limited to N5 vocabulary, but we have also included a few higher-level vocabulary if the word is extremely useful for the student. We have tried to indicate these non-N5 words when possible.

HOW TO USE THIS BOOK

This book offers three ways to practice reading Japanese for the N5 test:

1) 短文（80 文字） short paragraphs with about 80 characters followed by one or more questions for comprehension.

2) 中分 (250 文字) Mid-length paragraphs with about 250 characters followed by one or more questions for comprehension

3) 情報検索 In this section, you will be asked to extract necessary information using short text, graphs, or other visuals (such as timetables, schedules, or pamphlets).

SOUND FILES

While the reading section on the actual test does not have an audio component, we are including audio files for every essay and question. This is purely for extra practice. We recommend "shadowing" the text. Listen to the Japanese and then repeat it out loud. Pay attention to the pronunciation and intonation.

The download link at the end of this book includes MP3s for all the Japanese.

ABOUT CLAY & YUMI

Yumi was a popular radio DJ in Japan for over ten years. She has extensive training in standard Japanese pronunciation which makes her perfect for creating these language instructional audio files.

Clay has been a passionate learner of Japanese for over twenty years now. He started what became his free language learning website, www.TheJapanesePage.com, way back in 1999 as a sort of diary of what he was learning.

In 2002, he and Yumi began TheJapanShop.com as a way to help students of Japanese get hard-to-find Japanese books. Since then, they have written over twenty books on various Japanese language topics.

Yumi and I are **very grateful** for your purchase and we truly hope this book will help you improve your Japanese. **We love our customers and don't take a single one of you for granted.** If you have any questions about this book or Japanese in general, I invite you to contact us below by email or on social media.

CLAY & YUMI BOUTWELL (AND MAKOTO & MEGUMI)

help@thejapanshop.com

@theJapanShop

https://www.facebook.com/LearningJapaneseatTheJapanShop

http://www.TheJapanShop.com

CONTENTS

SECTION 1: SHORT PARAGRAPHS

短文（80 文字） short paragraphs

with about 80 characters followed by

one or more questions for

comprehension.

JOHN'S DIARY #1

ジョンさんが 書^かいた 日記^{にっき} #1 です。
読^よんで 質問^{しつもん}に 答^{こた}えて ください。

きのうは、としょかん に 行^いきました。本^{ほん}を たくさん 読^よみました。 でも、かりませんでした。かえりに、コンビニ^{こんびに}で ざっし とべんとう を かいました。日本^{にほん}の コンビニは、とても べんり です。

① きのう は、どこ へ 行^いきましたか？

A、コンビニ

B、としょかん

C、コンビニ と としょかん

D、学校^{がっこう}

② コンビニ で 何^{なに} を かいましたか？

A、ざっし

B、本^{ほん}

C、べんとう

D、ざっし と べんとう

GRAMMAR NOTES:

■ In the instructions, the phrase ジョンさんが 書いた 日記 is used. It means "the diary John wrote," but the literal order is "John-(subject marker)-wrote-diary." In Japanese, adjectives and verbs can be stacked behind nouns to further describe the noun: 半分 食べた ケーキ a half-eaten cake.

KEY VOCABULARY

- 書いた wrote [from 書く (to write)]

- 日記 diary [日 is a N5 kanji, but 記 is N3. 記 means "scribe" or "narrative"]

- 読んで please read [from 読む (to read)]

- 質問 question; problems [while both kanji are N4, the word and the kanji are common]

- としょかん library [the kanji is 図書館. Only 書 is N5 kanji]

- 本 book

- でも but; however

- かりません didn't borrow [from 借^かりる (to borrow or rent)]

- コンビニ convenience store

- かいました bought [from 買^かう (to buy)]

- 学校^{がっこう} school [both kanji are N5]

- べんとう lunchbox; bento [the kanji is 弁当^{べんとう}]

- ざっし magazine [the kanji is 雑誌^{ざっし}]

- とても very

- べんり convenient [kanji: 便利^{べんり} (both N3 kanji)]

ANSWERS:

1) C – He went to the library and a convenience store on his way home

2) D – He bought a magazine and a bento

JOHN'S DIARY #2

ジョンさんが 書いた 日記 #2 です。
読んで 質問に 答えて ください。

今日は、 あさ、 へや の そうじ を
しました。せんたく も しました。 天気 が
よかった ので、 せんたくもの が よく
かわきました。 ゆうがた は、 きんじょ を
さんぽ しました。しょうらい は、いぬ を
かって いっしょに さんぽ したい です。

① 今日は、あさ、何を しました か？

　　A、さんぽ

　　B、そうじ

　　C、そうじ と せんたく

　　D、せんたく

② ゆうがたは 何を しました か？

　　A、さんぽ

　　B、いぬ と さんぽ

　　C、せんたく

　　D、べんきょう

GRAMMAR NOTES:

■ かって　いっしょに　さんぽ　したい "to get a (pet) and then I want to walk with it." The て form of かう (to keep a pet) makes it a conjunction: "and then."

➢ 食べて　さんぽ　します eat **and then** take a walk [て form of 食べる]

➢ 日本語を　べんきょう　して　ねます to study Japanese **and then** go to sleep [て form of する]

KEY VOCABULARY:

- 今日 today [literally, "now day"]

- あさ morning [kanji: 朝]

- へや room [kanji: 部屋]

- そうじ cleaning [kanji: 掃除]

- へや　の　そうじ cleaning the room [the の connects and shows a relationship; think of it as an apostrophe S: room's cleaning]

- せんたく washing (clothes)

- せんたくもの laundry; the washing [literally, laundry thing]

- 天気 weather [天 (heaven; sky) + 気 (air)]

- よかった (weather was) good

- ので therefore; because of that

- よく (dried) well; (dried) nicely

- かわきました dried

- ゆうがた evening [kanji: 夕方]

- きんじょ neighborhood [kanji: 近所]

- さんぽ walk; go for a stroll [kanji: 散歩]

- しょうらい future [kanji: 将来]

- いぬ dog [kanji: 犬]

- かって keep (a pet) [*te* form of 飼う to domesticate; to raise; to keep (a pet); note this is a different word from 買う (to buy)]

- いっしょに together

- したい want to

ANSWERS:

1) C – He cleaned and washed

2) A – He went for a walk but doesn't have a dog yet.

JOHN'S DIARY #3

ジョンさんが 書いた 日記 #3 です。
読んで 質問に 答えて ください。

今日は、 学校に ちこく しました。あさ おきる のが すこし おそかった ので、バス に のれません でした。先生に おこられまし た。明日は、めざまし時計 を つかいます。

① ジョンさんは、どうして ちこく しました か？

A、バスが おくれた。

B、あさ、おきる のが おそかった。

C、先生に おこられた。

D、めざまし時計 が なかった。

GRAMMAR NOTES:

■ With のが, the の makes the preceding phrase into a noun phrase and が sets that noun phrase as the subject.

> あなたは　え　を　かく　のが　上手(じょうず)　です。
> [as for you – picture – (direct object marker) – drawing/painting – のが – good at]
> You are good at drawing pictures.

KEY VOCABULARY:

* 今日(きょう) today [literally, "now day"]

* 学校(がっこう) school [学 (study; learning) + 校 (school)]

* ちこく　late; tardy [kanji: 遅刻(ちこく); 遅 (slow) + 刻 (cut; engrave)]

* あさ morning [kanji: 朝(あさ)]

* おきる to get up; wake up [kanji: 起(お)きる]

* すこし a little [kanji: 少(すこ)し]

* おそかった was late [past of 遅(おそ)く late]

* ので therefore; because of that

- バス bus [from the English]

- のれません　でした didn't ride [from 乗^のる (to ride (vehicle))]

- 先生^{せんせい} teacher

- おこられました was scolded [passive form of 怒^{おこ}る (to get angry; to be mad)]

- 明日 tomorrow

- めざまし時計^{どけい} alarm clock [めざまし (waking up) + 時計^{とけい} (watch; clock)]

- つかいます to use [kanji: 使^{つか}う]

- どうして why

ANSWERS:

1) B – He slept late.

JOHN'S DIARY #4

ジョンさんが 書いた 日記 #4 です。
読んで 質問に 答えて ください。

今日と あしたは、学校が 休み です。
今日は、友だちと こうえんに 行きます。あし
たは、 山に 行きます。 あさ はやく おき
て、友だちと いっしょに のぼります。今夜
は、はやく ねます。

① 休みは いつ です か?

　A、今日 と あした

　B、きのう と 今日

　C、今日 だけ

　D、あした だけ

② あしたは、何を しますか?

　A、こうえん に 行く。

　B、学校 に 行く。

　C、山 に のぼる。

　D、ねる。

GRAMMAR NOTES:

■ The adverbs はやく (early) and おそく (late) can be added to time nouns. You will often hear these:

- ➢ あさ　はやく early in the morning
- ➢ よる　おそく late at night
- ➢ 毎(まい)あさ　はやく early every morning
- ➢ 毎(まい)ばん　おそく late every evening

KEY VOCABULARY:

- 今日(きょう) today [literally, "now day"]

- と and

- 明日(あした) tomorrow [明 (bright; light) + 日 (day; sun)]

- 学校(がっこう) school [学 (study; learning) + 校 (school)]

- 休(やす)み break (from school); rest; vacation [from 休(やす)む (rest; day off)]

- 友(とも)だち friend

- こうえん (public) park [kanji: 公園(こうえん)]

- 行(い)きます to go [dictionary form: 行(い)く (to go)]

- 山 <ruby>やま</ruby> mountain

- あさ morning

- はやく early; soon [this also can mean "quickly" or "fast"]

- あさ　はやく early in the morning

- おきて wake up and [from 起きる (to get up); the て form makes it into a conjunction]

- といっしょに together with [the person you are together with (in this case, a friend) is placed before the と]

- のぼります climb (mountain) [kanji: 登る (to climb; to ascend; to hike)]

- 今夜 this evening [今 (now) + 夜 (evening; night)]

- ねます sleep [kanji: 寝る (to sleep)]

ANSWERS:

1) A – John's day off is today and tomorrow.

2) C – He will climb a mountain tomorrow.

JOHN'S DIARY #5

ジョンさんが 書いた 日記 #5 です。
読んで 質問に 答えて ください。

今日は、 スーパーに かいもの に 行きました。まめ の かんづめ と パン を かいました。ブロッコリー と にんじん も かいました。さかな が セール で やすかった です。 でも、さかな が あまり 好きじゃない ので、かいません でした。

① スーパー で かわなかった もの は、何でしょう？

　　A、まめ の かんづめ

　　B、さかな

　　C、ブロッコリー と にんじん

　　D、何も かいません でした。

GRAMMAR NOTES:

■ さかな　が　<u>あまり</u>　すきじゃない　(I) don't like fish <u>very</u> much

> ➤ あまり（not very; not much）
> This is followed with a negative ender. In this case, すき<u>じゃない</u> (to <u>not</u> like).
>
> EXAMPLE:
> お客様は　あまり　いません　でした。
> There weren't many customers.

KEY VOCABULARY:

- 今日 today [literally, "now day"]
- スーパー supermarket [many Japanese words borrowed from English are abbreviated; while スーパー can be used to mean "super" as in スーパーマン (Superman), in general, this is used for "supermarket"]
- かいもの shopping [kanji: 買い物]
- 行きました went [past *masu* form of 行く (to go)]
- まめ beans; legume; peas [kanji: 豆]

- かんづめ canned food [kanji: 缶詰<ruby>かんづめ</ruby>; 缶 (tin can) + 詰 (packed; press in)]
- パン bread [from Portuguese]
- かいました bought [from 買<ruby>か</ruby>う (to buy)]
- ブロッコリー broccoli
- と and
- にんじん carrot [kanji: 人参<ruby>にんじん</ruby>]
- も also
- さかな fish [kanji: 魚<ruby>さかな</ruby>]
- セール sale [from English]
- やすかった was inexpensive [past of 安<ruby>やす</ruby>い (cheap; inexpensive)]
- でも but; however
- あまり not much; not very [used with a negative ending (didn't like)]
- 好<ruby>す</ruby>きじゃない didn't like [好<ruby>す</ruby>き (to like) + じゃない not]
- ので therefore; because of that

ANSWERS:

1) B – He isn't fond of fish.

JOHN'S DIARY #6

ジョンさんが 書いた 日記 #6 です。
読んで 質問に 答えて ください。

　　今日は、 たくさん の しゅくだい が 出ました。日本語 で てがみ を 書いて く ださい と いわれました。日本 の 友だち に 書きました。 それから 日本語 の あた らしい ことば を おぼえました。 かんじ も すこし おぼえました。

① どんな しゅくだい が でました か?
　A、日本語 で てがみ を 書いて くださ い。
　B、ひらがな を おぼえて ください。
　C、かんじ を かいて ください。
　D、きょうか書 を 読んで ください。
② だれに てがみ を 書きました?
　A、お母さん
　B、友だち
　C、先生
　D、じぶん

GRAMMAR NOTES:

■ Add ください after the て form of verbs to make a polite request:

> 食べて ください (please eat) [from 食べる (to eat)]

> べんきょう して ください (please study) [from 勉強する (to study)]

KEY VOCABULARY:

- 今日 today [literally, "now day"]

- たくさん many; much

- しゅくだい homework [kanji: 宿題; 宿 (lodge; home; dwell) + 題 (topic; subject)]

- 出ました put out; (homework) given [past of 出る (to appear; to come out)]

- 日本語 Japanese language [日 (day; sun) + 本 (origin) + 語 (word; language)]

- てがみ letter; correspondence [kanji: 手紙; 手 (hand) + 紙 (paper)]

- 書いてください please write [て form of 書く (to write) + ください (please)]

- といわれました was told [と (quotation marker) + passive of 言う (to speak; to say)]

- お母さん mother

- それから and then; after that

- あたらしい new [kanji: 新しい]

- ことば word [kanji: 言葉; this can also mean words, phrases, or language in general]

- おぼえました learned [from 覚える (to memorize; to learn)]

- かんじ kanji; Chinese characters used in Japanese [kanji: 漢字; 漢 (Sino-; China) + 字 (character; letter)]

- すこし a little [すこし　おぼえました　か？]

ANSWERS:

1) A – He had to write a letter in Japanese.
2) B – His Japanese friend.

THIS WEEK'S SALE

ジョンさんが 書_かいた 日記_{にっき} #7 です。
読_よんで 質問_{しつもん}に 答_{こた}えて ください。

　今_{こん}しゅう の セールは とうふ と チョコ
レート です。 先_{せん}しゅう より やすい で
す。 とうふは 100円_{ひゃくえん}、 そして チョコレート
は ５０円_{ごじゅうえん} です。とうふ 1_{いっ}こ と チョコレ
ート 2_にこを かいました。たまねぎも ほしか
った、けど わすれました。

① 今日は、何_{なに} を かいました か？
　　A、とうふ と チョコレート と たまねぎ
　　B、たまねぎ だけ
　　C、とうふ と チョコレート 2_にこ
　　D、ぜんぶ わすれました

② いくら はらいましたか？
　　A、100 円
　　B、200 円
　　C、300 円
　　D、1000 円

GRAMMAR NOTES:

■ 先しゅう　<u>より</u>　やすい　です。 Cheaper <u>than</u> last week.

The より shows the topic is more or greater than the word that comes before より.

> ➢ 今日は　きのう　より　あつい　です。 Today is hotter than yesterday. [Literally: as for today – yesterday – (more) than – hot – is]

KEY VOCABULARY:

- 今しゅう this week [kanji: 今週; 今 (this; now; at the moment) + 周 (week)]

- セール sale

- とうふ fermented bean curd [kanji: 豆腐; 豆 (bean; pea) + 腐 (rot; decay; sour)]

- と and

- チョコレート chocolate

- 先しゅう last week [kanji: 先週; 先 (before; ahead; previous; future; precedence) + 周 (week)]

- 先_{せん}しゅうよりやすい even cheaper than last week [せんしゅう (last week) + より (than; is placed after what the following is compared to) + やすい (cheap; inexpensive)]

- そして and; and then

- かいました bought [polite past tense form of the verb 買_かう (to buy; to purchase)]

- いえ house; residence; dwelling [kanji: 家_{いえ} (house; home; family; professional; expert; performer)]

- かえって returning [from 帰_{かえ}る (to return)]

- から after (returning)

- たまねぎ onion [kanji: 玉葱_{たまねぎ}]

- わすれました forgot [polite past tense form of the verb 忘_{わす}れる (to forget; to leave carelessly; to be forgetful of)]

ANSWERS:

1) C – He bought both sale items.
2) B – 100 + 50 + 5

JAPANESE TEA

読んで 質問に 答えて ください。

　　日本人は、おちゃ が 大すき です。しょくじ の 時、おちゃを のむ 人 が おおい です。ウーロンちゃ や むぎちゃ も のみます。さとう や ミルク は 入れません。おちゃ は、からだ に いい です。日本人は、おちゃ を たくさん のみます。コンビニ でも いろんな おちゃ が うっています。　　　・

① 日本人は おちゃに なにを いれます か？
　A、なにも いれません
　B、ミルク
　C、さとう
　D、ミルク と さとう

GRAMMAR NOTES:

■ Add 大 (big) before certain nouns to make the meaning "bigger":

> 大好き love; like very much [big + like]

> 大会 convention [big + meeting]

> 大学 university [big + learning/school]

> 大人 adult (note the irregular pronunciation "*otona*") [big + person]

> 大事 important; serious [big + thing]

KEY VOCABULARY:

- 日本人 Japanese person; Japanese people [日 (day; sun; counter for days) + 本 (book; present; main; origin; true; real) + 人 (person)]

- おちゃ tea [kanji: お茶]

- 大すき like very much [kanji: 大好き; 大 (large; big) + 好き (like; favorite)]

- しょくじ meal [kanji: 食事; 食 (food; eat) + 事 (matter; thing; fact); somewhat formal]

- 時 (specified) time; when; during

- おちゃをのむ人 a person who drinks tea [おちゃ (tea) + を (direct object marker) のむ (to drink) + 人 (person)]

- おおい many; numerous; a lot [kanji: 多い]

- ウーロンちゃ oolong tea

- や and; or

- むぎちゃ barley tea [kanji: 麦茶]

- も also; too

- のみます to drink [polite present tense form of the verb 飲む (to drink; to gulp]

- さとう sugar [kanji: 砂糖]

- ミルク milk

- 入れません do not put in [polite negative form (*masen*-form) of the verb 入れる (to put in)]

- からだにいい good for the body; healthy [からだ (body) + に (indicates the receiver of "good") + いい (good)]

- たくさん a lot; plenty; many

- コンビニ convenience store

- いろんな various [kanji: 色_{いろ}んな]

- うっています is selling [present progressive tense of the verb 売る（to sell）]

ANSWERS:

1) A – No milk or sugar please.

BENTO

読んで 質問に 答えて ください。

日本 では、たくさん の 人 が おべんとう を 食べます。おべんとうやさん や コンビニ には、いろいろな おべんとう が うっています。 とても べんり です。

わかい お母さんたちは、のり や たまご を つかって かわいい おべんとう を つくります。子どもたちは、とても すき です。

えき には、「えき べん」という おべんとう が うっています。日本では どこでも おべんとう が あります。

① おべんとうは　どこに　あります　か？

　　A、いえ　だけ

　　B、コンビニ　だけ

　　C、おべんとうやさん　だけ

　　D、どこでも

② わかい　お母<ruby>母<rt>かあ</rt></ruby>さんたちは　どう　やって　かわ
いい　おべんとうを　つくります　か？

　　A、えきべんを　つかいます。

　　B、のり　や　たまごを　つかいます。

　　C、こどもが　つくります。

　　D、おべんとうは　かわいくない　です。

GRAMMAR NOTES:

■ のり　や　たまご　を　つかって　かわいい
おべんとう　を　つくります。

Add seaweed or eggs and make a cute bento.

The て form of the verb つかって makes it into a
conjunction: use (seaweed or eggs) *and* …. This is used
to add details to the sentence and isn't used for contrast.

> 食べて　ねる。 eat and (then) sleep [from 食べ
> る (to eat) + 寝る (to sleep)]

> べんきょう　して　しけん　を　うける。
> Study and take a test [from 勉強する (to study)
> + 試験を受ける to take a test]

KEY VOCABULARY:

- 日本 Japan [日 (day; sun) + 本 (origin; book)]

- たくさん many; a lot

- 人 person

- おべんとう Japanese box lunch [kanji: お弁当]

- 食べます to eat [polite present tense form of the verb 食べる (to eat)]

- おべんとうやさん a shop selling take-away lunches; lunch box store [kanji: お弁当屋; お弁当 (lunch box) + 屋 (shop)]

- や and [used when listing items for examples]

- コンビニ convenience store

- いろいろ variety of; various; all sorts of [kanji: 色々]

- うっています is selling [present progressive tense of the verb 売る (to sell)]

- とても very; exceedingly

- べんり convenient; handy [kanji: 便利]

- わかい young; youthful [kanji: 若い]

- お母さんたち mothers; moms [turns the noun お母さん (mother) to plural form, by adding たち (pluralizing suffix)]

- のり edible seaweed

- や and

- たまご egg [kanji: 卵]

- つかって using [it is a て form (connective form of the verb) of the verb 使う (to use)]

- かわいい cute; adorable; charming [kanji: 可愛い]

- つくります to make; to create [polite present tense form of the verb 作る (to make)]

- 子どもたち children [turns the noun 子供 (child) to plural form, by adding たち (pluralizing suffix)]

- すき like; favorite [kanji: 好き]

- えき train station; railway station [kanji: 駅]

- という called; named [と (quotation marker) + 言う (say; call)]

- どこでも anywhere

ANSWERS:

1) D – Anywhere

2) B – Add things like seaweed or eggs to make it cute.

SECTION 2: LONGER PARAGRAPHS

中分 (250 文字) Mid-length paragraphs

with about 250 characters followed by one

or more questions for comprehension

MEDICINE

つぎの　ぶんを　よんで、　しつもんに　こたえて　ください。

　けさ、　あたま　が　いたかった　ので　くすりを　のみました。食べもの　と　いっしょに　のんだ　ほう　が　いい　ので　おひるごはん　の　あと　に　のみました。

　ちょっと　よく　なりました　が、　三時間後また　あたま　が　いたく　なりました。その　くすり　は　一日に　三かい　まで　のんでも　いい　と　かいて　ありました。それで　もう　いちど　くすり　を　のみました。そして　ひるねを　しました。

　３０ぷん後に　おきました。あたまは　もう　いたく　ありません　でした。

　その後　外へ　行きました。天気が　よかったです。そらも　きれい　でした。

　たぶん　くすり　だけ　では　よく　なりません　でした。ひるね　も　たいせつ　です。

① けさ、どこが　いたかった　ですか？

    A、おなか

    B、あたま

    C、め

    D、あし

② くすりは、一日で　何かい　のんでも　いいです　か？

    A、いっかい　だけ

    B、二かい

    C、三かい

    D、五かい

GRAMMAR NOTES:

■ Use もう (already; (not) anymore) to show something has already been done in time (past) or is no longer needed.

> ➤ もう　食べました。　(I've) already eaten.
> ➤ もう　べんきょう　できません。(I) can't study anymore.

■ Also, もう can also be used with time (future/present) to mean "now" or "soon."

> ➤ もう　すぐ　きます。(He'll) come soon. [Note: this could also mean "I'll come soon."]
> ➤ もう　そろそろ　かえりましょう。Let's go home soon (about now).

■ Lastly, もう can also be used to mean "more" or "another."

> ➤ もう　一ど　言って　ください。Please say that again.
> ➤ かみを　もう　一まい　ください。Please give (me) one more piece of paper. [literally: paper – (direct object marker) – another – one piece –

44

please; まい is the counter for flat objects like paper.]

KEY VOCABULARY:

- けさ this morning [kanji: 今朝; 今 (this; now) + 朝 (morning)]

- あたま head [kanji: 頭]

- いたかった was painful [past tense form of I-adjective 痛い (painful; sore)]

- ので because

- くすり medicine [kanji: 薬]

- のみました drank; took (medicine) [from 飲む (to drink)]

- 食べもの food

- いっしょに together with [kanji: 一緒に]

- のんだほうがいい it would be better to drink [飲んだ (past-casual form of the verb 飲む) + ほう

がいい, is used to suggest that a certain option is better]

- おひるごはん lunch; midday meal [kanji: お昼ご飯; お昼 (noon) + ご飯 (meal)]

- あと later; after [kanji: 後]

- ちょっと a bit; slightly; a little bit

- よく　なりました have become better

- が but; however

- 後 after

- まだ still

- その that (something or someone distant from the speaker, close to the listener)

- 一日 one day

- まで until; up to

- いい good; sufficient; enough

- もういちど again; once more

- そして and then; and

- ひるね nap (afternoon) [kanji: 昼寝; 昼 (daytime; noon) + 寝 (sleep)]

- その後 after that; afterwards; thereafter

- 外 outside; open air

- 天気 weather [天 (heaven; sky) + 気 (air; atmosphere)]

- きれい fair; beautiful; lovely [kanji: 綺麗]

- たぶん probably; maybe; perhaps

- だけ only; merely

- よく　なりません will not recover [polite negative form of よくなる (to become better; to recover)

- たいせつ important; necessary [kanji: 大切]

ANSWERS:

1) B – Headache

2) C – The medicine may be taken three times.

MY DOG

つぎの ぶんを よんで、 しつもんに こたえて ください。

わたし の いぬ の 名前 は ポチ で
す。あまり 大きく ありません。ねこ ぐらい
の 大きさで、とても かわいいです。

きのう、ポチ と さんぽ に 行きました。
とちゅうで 大きいな ねこ が いました。
ポチ より おおきかった です。でも、ポチ
は その ねこ まで はしりました。ねこが
にげた ので、ポチは ずっと とおく まで
はしりました。その ねこは 木に のぼりまし
た。それから ポチは その木の下で わんわん
と なきました。

ポチは、ねこ が すき では ありません.

① いぬは、どの　くらい　の　大_{おお}きさ　ですか？

　　A、ねこ　より　大_{おお}きい

　　B、ねこ　くらい　の　大_{おお}きさ

　　C、とても　大_{おお}きい

　　D、とても　小_{ちい}さい

② ポチは、ねこ　が　すき　ですか？

　　A、すこし　すき。

　　B、わからない

　　C、あまり　すき　では　ありません

　　D、大_{だい}すき

GRAMMAR NOTES:

■ くらい (also pronounced ぐらい) means "approximately" or "about." This is often used when comparing or estimating.

> ➤ どの くらい いた の？ How long did you stay? [The の is a casual question marker; いた is past of いる (to be; to stay)]

> ➤ いっしゅうかん ぐらい About one week.

> ➤ かのじょは、４０さい ぐらい です。 She is about 40.

KEY VOCABULARY:

- わたしの my [kanji: 私 (I; me) + の (possessive marker)]

- いぬ dog [kanji: 犬]

- 名前 name

- ポチ Pochi [a common "generic" dog name in Japanese; like Spot or Rover]

- 大^{おお}きく　ありません small; is not big [polite present negative form of 大^{おお}きいです (is big)]

- ねこ cat [kanji: 猫^{ねこ}]

- ぐらい about; approximately; around

- 大^{おお}きさ size

- とても very; exceedingly

- かわいい cute; adorable; lovely [kanji: 可愛^{か わい}い]

- きのう yesterday [kanji: 昨日^{き の う}; 昨 (last) + 日 (day)]

- さんぽ walk; stroll [kanji: 散歩^{さん ぽ}]

- 行^いきました went [polite past tense form of the verb 行^いく (to go; to move)]

- とちゅうで on the way [kanji: 途中^{と ちゅう}; 途 (route; way; road) + 中 (middle)]

- より　おおきかった was bigger than [大^{おお}きかった is a past form of i-adjective 大^{おお}きい (big); より +adjective means than/more than]

- でも but; however

- その that (something or someone distant from the speaker, close to the listener)

- まで to; up to

- はしりました ran [polite past tense form of the verb 走る (to run)]

- その that (something or someone distant from the speaker, close to the listener)

- 木 tree

- ので because

- 木の下 under the tree

- わんわん bow-wow (dog's barking sound)

- なきました cried; barked [used with animals and birds]

ANSWERS:

1) B – About the size of a cat.

2) C – The dog doesn't like cats.

TRIP TO JAPAN

つぎの　ぶんを　よんで、しつもんに　こたえて　ください。

　去年、わたし　の　かぞく　は　日本へ　りょこう　に　行きました。わたし　の　かぞく　は　4人　です。　父、母、いもうと、と　わたしです。りょこう　の　前に、毎日　日本語を　べんきょう　しました。だから、　すこし　日本語が　できます。

　ひこうきに　のっている　時間　が　とても　長かった　ですが、たのしかった　です。　日本に　行く　ので、わくわく　しました。

　日本　では　ふじ山　に　のぼりました。東京　の　はらじゅく　と　しぶや　に　行きました。ぎんざ　で　いもうとが　かい物を　しました。

① なん人　日本に　行きましたか？

A、ひとりだけ

B、わたし　と　りょうしん

C、かぞく　ぜんいん

D、5人

② ぎんざで　いもうとは　なにを　しましたか？

A、ひこうきに　のりました。

B、日本語　の　べんきょうを　しました。

C、わくわくしました。

D、かい物を　しました。

GRAMMAR NOTES:

■ Using 前に (before…) [Add a の if placed after a noun; when placed after verbs, use the dictionary (plain) form.]

- 食べる　前に　手を　あらいましょう。Wash your hands before eating.
- 4年　前に　学生　でした。(I) was a student four years ago.
- 休みの　前に　すこし　べんきょう　します。Before taking a break, I will study a little.

KEY VOCABULARY:

- 去年 last year [去 (past; gone) + 年 (year)]
- わたし I; me [kanji: 私]
- かぞく family; members of a family [kanji: 家族]
- 日本 Japan [日 (day; sun) + 本 (origin; book)]
- りょこう travel; trip; journey [kanji: 旅行]

- 行きました went [polite past tense form of the verb 行く (to go)]

- 父 father

- 母 mother

- いもうと younger sister [kanji: 妹]

- 前に before

- 毎日 every day

- 日本語 Japanese language [日 (day; sun) + 本 (origin) + 語 (word; language)]

- べんきょう study [kanji: 勉強]

- だから therefore; so

- すこし a little

- できます to be able to do [polite present form of the verb 出来る]

- ひこうき airplane [kanji: 飛行機]

- のっている riding [present progressive tense of the verb 乗る (to ride)]

- 時間 time

- とても very; exceedingly

- 長^{なが}かった was long [past of i-adjective 長^{なが}い (long)]

- が but; however

- たのしかった it was fun [past of i-adjective 楽^{たの}しい (fun; enjoyable; pleasant)]

- 行^いく to go

- ので because

- わくわく excited; thrilled [onomatopoeia; indicates your heart is pounding with excitement]

- ふじ山^{さん} Mount Fuji

- のぼりました climbed [polite past tense form of the verb 登^{のぼ}る (to climb; to hike up (the mountain))]

- 東京^{とうきょう} Tokyo

- はらじゅく Harajuku (a place in Tokyo famous for gathering of cosplayers)

- しぶや Shibuya (a place in Tokyo known as a major commercial and business center, it houses the two busiest railway stations in the world, Shinjuku Station (southern half) and Shibuya Station.

- ぎんざ Ginza (Ginza is a popular shopping area of Tokyo with numerous internationally renowned department stores, boutiques, restaurants and coffeehouses—like Fifth Avenue in New York City. It is considered one of the most expensive, elegant, and luxurious streets in the world)

- かい物 shopping

ANSWERS:

1) C – All four members of the family.

2) D – She shopped in Ginza.

MOUNTAIN

つぎの ぶんを よんで、しつもんに こたえて ください。

　あしたは、友だち と いっしょに 山に の
ぼります。あさ 8時に ちかく の えき で
友だち に あいます。電車で ３０分 の と
ころに 山 の のぼり口 が あります。山
の 上 まで、1時間 ほど かかる そう で
す。

　友だち と 電話 で 話して、おべんとう
を もって いく こと に しました。わたし
は、コンビニ で サンドイッチ を かって
もって いく こと に します。友だちは、
じぶんで おにぎり を つくります。山 の
上は、すこし さむい ので、うわぎを もって
いきます。ぼうし も かぶった ほう が い
い と 友だち が 言いました。おちゃ か、
水 を もって 行きます。山 の 上 は と
ても きれい だ そう です。じぶん の 国
では、山 に のぼった こと が ない の
で、とても たのしみ に しています。

① あしたは、何を もって いきますか？

   A、べんとう

   B、サンドイッチ と 水 か おちゃ

   C、うわぎ と ぼうし

   D、A から C まで ぜんぶ

② 山 の 上は…

   A、すこし さむい

   B、すこし あつい

   C、高い

   D、ちかい

GRAMMAR NOTES:

■ ちかく　の　えき The nearby (train) station

Use this construction to show distance from something.

> ちかく　の　レストラン　a nearby restaurant [近く near; in the neighborhood]

> とおく　の　友だち　a faraway friend [遠く far away; distant]

KEY VOCABULARY:

- あした tomorrow [kanji: 明日]

- 友だち friend; companion [kanji: 友達]

- いっしょに together with [kanji: 一緒に]

- 山 mountain

- のぼります to climb; to go up [polite present tense form of the verb 登る (to climb)]

- あさ morning [kanji: 朝]

- ちかく near; neighborhood; vicinity [kanji: 近く]

- えき railway station; train station [kanji: 駅]

- 電車 train; electric train

- のぼり口 starting point for an ascent (mountain, stairs, etc.); base (of mountain, etc.) [kanji: 登り口; 登り (climb) + 口 (mouth)]

- 上 top

- ほど about (indicates approximate amount or maximum)

- かかる it takes

- そう they say…; I heard… [indicates second-hand information]

- 電話 phone call

- 話して talking; speaking [て form of the verb 話す (to talk; to speak), indicates connective form]

- おべんとう Japanese box lunch [kanji: お弁当]

- もって いく to take; to bring; to carry (something) away [kanji: 持って行く; 持つ (to hold) + 行く (to go somewhere)]

- こと に なりました it turned out that...; we decided that…

- わたし I; me [kanji: 私]

- コンビニ convenience store

- サンドイッチ sandwich

- かって もって いく buy and take away [買って (て form of the verb 買う (buy), a connective form of the verb) + 持って行く (take away)]

- じぶん myself; oneself [kanji: 自分]

- おにぎり onigiri; rice ball (often triangular, sometimes with a filling and wrapped in edible seaweed) [kanji: お握り]

- つくります to make [kanji: 作ります; polite present tense form of the verb 作る (to make)]

- 山の上 top of the mountain [山 (mountain); 上 (top)]

- すこし a little bit

- さむい cold (e.g. weather)

- ので because

- うわぎ jacket; coat [kanji: 上着; 上 (top; over) + 着 (clothes)]

- もって　いきます to take; to carry (something) away [kanji: 持って行きます; 持つ (to hold) + 行く (to go somewhere)；行きます is a polite present form of the verb 行く (to go)]

- ぼうし cap; hat [kanji: 帽子]

- も also; too

- かぶった wore; had put on [casual past tense form of the verb 被る (to put on one's head)]

- ほうがいい it would be better [is used to suggest that a certain option is better]

- いいました said [polite past tense form of the verb 言う (to say)]

- おちゃ tea [kanji: お茶]

- 水 water

- きれい fair; beautiful; lovely [kanji: 綺麗]

- 国 country

- 今まで so far; up to the present

- たのしみ　に　しています looking forward to [set phrase from 楽しむ (to delight; have joy]

ANSWERS:

1) D – Bring everything.
2) A – It's a little cold.

CUPCAKES

つぎの　ぶんを　よんで、しつもんに　こたえて　ください。

　　今日は、　友だち　と　カップケーキ　を　つくります。学校　の　クラス　の　みんなに　あげる　ので、たくさん　つくります。クラスには、１２人　の　友だち　が　います。

　　クラス　の　８人は　チョコレートカップケーキ　が　ほしい　と　言いました。　あとは　バニラ　カップケーキ　が　食べたい　そうです。

　　わたしは、たまご　と　ベーキングパウダーを　かいます。友だちが　バター　と　こむぎこを　かいます。

　　３時に　友だちが　くる　ので、今から　かいに　行きます。ちかく　の　スーパー　で　ちょうど　セールを　している　ので、たくさん　かいます。

　　おいしい　カップケーキを　つくりたい　です。

① 今日_{きょう}は、今_{いま}から　何_{なに}を　しますか？

　A、カップケーキを　つくる

　B、友達　と　あそぶ

　C、プレゼントを　つくる

　D、たまごを　わる

② 友_{とも}だちは　何_{なに}を　かいますか？

　A、バター

　B、こむぎこ

　C、バター　と　こむぎこ

　D、チョコレート

③ バニラが　ほしい　のは　何人_{なんにん}　ですか？

　A、１２人_{じゅうににん}

　B、８人_{はちにん}

　C、４人_{よにん}

　D、１人_{ひとり}

GRAMMAR NOTES:

■ The と in the following means "with" and not "and."

友<ruby>とも</ruby>だち　と　カップケーキ　を　つくります。

Otherwise, it would mean "(I) am making friends *and* cupcakes." Instead, it should be "(I) am making cupcakes *with* a friend."

> あの人<ruby>ひと</ruby>　と　話<ruby>はな</ruby>しました。　I talked *with* that person.

> かれは　わたし　と　いっしょに　りょこう した。　He traveled with me.

> だれ　と　話<ruby>はな</ruby>しました　か？　*With* whom did you speak? [or "Who did you speak *with*?"]

KEY VOCABULARY:

• 今日<ruby>きょう</ruby> today [literally, "now day"]

• 友<ruby>とも</ruby>だち friend; companion [kanji: 友達<ruby>ともだち</ruby>]

• と with

• カップケーキ cupcake

• つくります to make [kanji: 作<ruby>つく</ruby>ります; polite present tense form of the verb 作<ruby>つく</ruby>る (to make)]

- 学校〔がっこう〕 school

- クラス class

- みんなに to everyone; to all

- あげる give

- ので because

- たくさん many; a lot

- チョコレート chocolate

- バニラ vanilla

- わたし I; me [kanji: 私〔わたし〕]

- たまご egg [kanji: 卵〔たまご〕]

- ベーキング　パウダー baking powder

- かいます to buy; to purchase [polite present form of the verb 買〔か〕う]

- バター butter

- こむぎこ wheat flour [kanji: 小麦粉〔こむぎこ〕]

- きます to come [polite present tense form of the verb 来〔く〕る (to come)]

- ので because

- 今〔いま〕から from now; hence

- かいに　行きます go to buy [Verb-ます stem + に行く means to go in order to do something; かい is the ます stem of the verb 買う (to buy)]

- ちかく near; neighborhood; vicinity [kanji: 近く]

- スーパー supermarket

- ちょうど just; exactly; right; precisely; happens to be (on sale)

- セール sale

- ところ [Verb-て form + いる　ところ means in the process of doing]

- たくさん many; a lot

- 食べたい want to eat

ANSWERS:

1) A – They will make cupcakes.

2) C – His friend will bring butter and flour.

3) C – 8 classmates want chocolate, so 4 want vanilla

MY APARTMENT

つぎの ぶんを よんで、 しつもんに こたえて ください。

　　わたし の アパートは とても べんりな ところ に あります。まち の 中(なか) です が しずか です。となりに 小(ちい)さい こうえん が あります。みち の むこう には パンやさん が あります。ちかくに ぎんこう と スーパーが あります。

　　毎(まい)あさ、アパート から 大学(だいがく)に 行(い)きます。車(くるま)で 5分(ごふん) かかります。今日(きょう)は、学校(がっこう)から かえったら パンやさんに 行(い)きたい です。その パンやさんは いつも おいしい アンパンを つくっています。 食(しょく)パンも とても おいしい です。

　　ゆうがた、こうえんで 友(とも)だちと あいます。いっしょに パンやさんに 行(い)って、アンパンを 2(ふた)つ かいます。

71

① アパートから　ちかい　のは、何でしょう？

A、こうえん

B、ぎんこう

C、パンや

D、A,B,C　ぜんぶ

② 今日は　何を　かいますか？

A.　アンパン

B.　食パン

C.　さかな

D.　たこやき

GRAMMAR NOTES:

■ みち　の　むこう On the other side of the street

(Place or thing) の (direction or distance)

> ➤ いえ　は　はし　の　むこう　に　あります。
>
> (My) house is on the other side of the bridge.

> ➤ スーパー　の　みぎがわ to the right of the
>
> supermarket

KEY VOCABULARY:

- わたし　の　my [kanji: 私 (わたし) (I; me) + の (possessive marker)]

- アパート apartment

- とても very; exceedingly

- べんり convenient; handy [kanji: 便利 (べんり)]

- まち　の　中 (なか) in the town [kanji: 町 (まち) の中 (なか)]

- が but; however

- しずかな quiet; silent [kanji: 静 (しず) か]

- ところ place

- となり　に in the immediate vicinity [kanji: <ruby>隣<rt>となり</rt></ruby> に]

- <ruby>小<rt>ちい</rt></ruby>さい small; little; tiny

- こうえん (public park) [kanji: <ruby>公園<rt>こうえん</rt></ruby>]

- あります to exist; have [polite present tense form of the verb <ruby>有<rt>あ</rt></ruby>る (to exist)]

- みち road; path [kanji: <ruby>道<rt>みち</rt></ruby>]

- むこう opposite side; other side [kanji: <ruby>向<rt>む</rt></ruby>こう]

- パンや bakery [kanji: パン<ruby>屋<rt>や</rt></ruby>]

- ちかくに at a nearby site; in the vicinity [kanji: <ruby>近<rt>ちか</rt></ruby>くに]

- ぎんこう bank [kanji: <ruby>銀行<rt>ぎんこう</rt></ruby>]

- と and

- スーパー supermarket

- <ruby>毎<rt>まい</rt></ruby>あさ every morning [kanji: <ruby>毎朝<rt>まいあさ</rt></ruby>; 毎 (every) + 朝 (morning)]

- から from

- <ruby>大学<rt>だいがく</rt></ruby> university; college

- 行<ruby>い</ruby>きます　to go [dictionary form: 行<ruby>い</ruby>く (to go)]

- 車<ruby>くるま</ruby>で by car

- かかります it takes [dictionary form: かかる (it takes)]

- かえったら when (I) get back; when (I) return

- 行<ruby>い</ruby>きたい want to go

- その that (something or someone distant from the speaker, close to the listener)

- いつも always; usually

- おいしい delicious; tasty [kanji: 美味<ruby>おい</ruby>しい]

- アンパン anpan; bread roll filled with red bean paste

- つくっています is making [polite present progressive tense of the verb 作<ruby>つく</ruby>る (to make)]

- それと and then

- 食<ruby>しょく</ruby>パン (loaf of) bread

- かいたい want to buy [kanji: 買<ruby>か</ruby>いたい; 買い + たい expresses desire to buy; 〜たい means "to want to do"]

- ゆうがた evening; dusk [kanji: 夕方]

- 友だち friend; companion [kanji: 友達]

- かいます to buy; to purchase [polite present tense form of the verb 買う (to buy)]

ANSWERS:

1) D – All of the above

2) A – He bought two anpans.

SECTION 3: INFORMATION

情報検索 In this section, you will be asked to extract necessary information using short text, graphs, or other visuals (such as timetables, schedules, or pamphlets).

CUPCAKE

つぎの ぶんを よんで、しつもんに こたえて ください。

カップケーキ の レシピ（5人ぶん）

こむぎこ	100グラム
バター	50グラム
たまご	1こ
ぎゅうにゅう	60CC
ベーキング パウダー	小さじ1

① こむぎこ と バターは、あわせて 何グラム に なります か？

    A、100グラム

    B、50グラム

    C、150グラム

    D、1000グラム

② 20人ぶん の カップケーキを つくる とき、たまごは、いくつ に なります か？

    A、4

    B、3

    C、2

    D、1

GRAMMAR NOTES:

■ に　なります is a versatile word that shows the results of a change: become; get; grow; attain; result in; etc.

- ４０さい　に　なりました。(I) turned 40.
- 友だち　に　なりましょう。Let's become friends. [なりましょう means "let's become"]
- 大きく　なった！(You've) grown so big! [often said to children.]
- しずか　に　なりました。(It) became quiet.

KEY VOCABULARY:

- カップケーキ cupcake
- レシピ recipe
- ５人　ぶん five person's portion
- こむぎこ wheat flour [kanji: 小麦粉]
- グラム gram
- バター butter
- たまご egg [kanji: 卵]

- こ piece [kanji: 個 (counter for articles)]

- ぎゅうにゅう (cow's) milk [kanji: 牛乳 ; 牛 (cow) + 乳 (milk)]

- CC cubic centimeter

- ベーキング　パウダー baking powder

- 小さじ 1 one teaspoon

- 荷グラム how many grams

- に　なります　か will it be?

- いくら how much?; how many?

ANSWERS:

1) C – 100 + 50

2) A – 1 egg for 5 people, so 4 eggs for 20.

THIS WEEK'S SALES

つぎの　ぶんを　よんで、　しつもんに　こたえて　ください。

こんしゅう　の　セール

月よう日

みかん　1こ　30円
　　　　10こ　270円

火よう日

きゅうり　1本　100円
　　　　　5本　450円

水よう日

チョコレート　1こ　80円
　　　　　　　10こ　720円

チョコレートを　10こ　かう　と、マシュマロ
を　1こ　プレゼント　します。

① チョコレートを　かう　なら、何よう日　が
いい　です　か？

    A、月曜日

    B、火曜日

    C、水曜日

    D、日曜日

② 月よう日に、ミカン　１０こは　いくら　にな
りますか？

    A、７３０円

    B、１００円

    C、２７０円

    D、７２０円

GRAMMAR NOTES:

■ Common Counters

Using counters gives us information about the objects we are counting.

■ 人 counter for people

■ 歳 counter for ages of people and animals; this is also written as 才; this is fairly regular except for age 20 which is はたち.

■ 個 counter for small or round objects [fruits; eggs]

■ 本 counter for long, cylindrical objects [bottles; pencils; chopsticks]

■ 枚 counter for flat, thin objects [sheets of paper; stamps; plates; shirts]

■ 匹 counter for small animals [cats; dogs; fish—usually up to the size of a dog. For larger animals, 頭 is used.]

■ 冊 counter for books

There are many, many more, but these are of the most useful.

KEY VOCABULARY:

- こんしゅう this week [kanji: 今週; 今 (this) + 週 (week)]

- 月よう日 Monday

- みかん citrus; satsuma mandarin

- 一こ one piece [kanji: 一個 (counter for articles)]

- ３０円 thirty yen [円 is Japanese monetary unit]

- 火よう日 Tuesday

- 水よう日 Wednesday

- きゅうり cucumber [kanji: 胡瓜]

- 1本 one piece [本 is counter for long cylindrical thing]

- チョコレート chocolate

- かう buy [kanji: 買う]

- と if; upon (buying ten chocolates)

- マシュマロ marshmallow

- プレゼント presents; gift

- なら if; in case

- 何ようび what day?; what day of the week?

- いい good; fine; nice; OK

ANSWERS:

1) C – Chocolate is on sale on Wednesday.

2) C – Oranges are even cheaper when buying 10 of them.

SCHOOL OUTING

つぎの　ぶんを　よんで、しつもんに　こたえて　ください。

今月は、３０日（火よう日）に　学校　の
りょこう　が　あります。クラス　の　みんな
で　海に　行きます。きて　ください。

どこ：しらはま　の　海
いつ：７月３０日（火よう日）

おべんとう　を　わすれないで　ください。

　１５日　までに　先生に　おしえて　くださ
い。
　お金を　もって　きて　もいい　です　が、な
くさないで　ください。
　たのしい　一日に　しましょう。

① お金を　もって　きて　も　いい　です　か？

　　A、だめ　です。

　　B、もって　きて　も　いい　です。

　　C、たくさん　もって　きて　ください

　　D、１００円　だけ

② どこへ　行きます　か？

　　A、学校

　　B、海

　　C、先生　の　家

　　D、山

GRAMMAR NOTES:

■ お金<ruby>かね</ruby>を　もって　きて　もいい　です。(You) may bring money.

The 〜てもいい construction means "you may" or "it is allowed." Tack もいい (also okay) after the て form of a verb to make that act permissible:

> 食<ruby>た</ruby>べても　いい　です　か？　Is it all right to eat?
> しつもん　しても　いい　です　か？ May I ask a question?
> どっち　でも　いい　です。Either way is fine.
> なんでも　いい　です。Anything is fine.

You can also use it with a negative to mean "there's no need" or "you don't have to…"

> きんちょう　しなくても　いい　です　よ。There's no need to be that tense.
> おさけを　のまなくても　いい　です。You don't have to drink sake. [The お before さけ is polite language]

KEY VOCABULARY:

- 今月 this month [今 (now) + 月 (month)]

- ３０日 thirtieth day of the month

- 火よう日 Tuesday

- 学校 school

- りょこう travel; excursion; trip

- クラス class

- みんな all; everyone; everybody

- 海 sea; ocean

- 行きます to go [polite present tense of the verb 行く (to go)]

- きて　ください please come [来て is the て form of the verb 来る (to come); Verb-て form + ください means "please do something"]

- どこ where

- いつ when

- 海 (うみ) sea; ocean

- 7 月 (しちがつ) July

- おべんとう Japan lunchbox [kanji: お弁当 (べんとう)]

- わすれないで　ください please don't forget; please remember [from 忘れる (わすれる) (to forget); Verb-command negative form + ないでください means "please don't do"]

- 1 5 日 (にち) fifteenth day of the month

- までに not later than; by

- 先生 (せんせい) teacher; instructor

- おしえて　ください please tell [from 教える (おしえる) (to tell; to teach); Verb て form + ください means "please do something"]

- お金 (かね) money

- もって　きて　も　いい　です it is OK to bring along [Verb て form + もいいです is used to express politely that it is OK to do something]

- が but; however

- なくさないで　ください please don't lose [from なくす (to lose); Verb-command negative form + ないでください means "please don't do"]

- たのしい fun; enjoyable; pleasant [kanji: 楽^{たの}しい]

- 一日^{いちにち} one day

- しましょう let's do it; will do [polite volitional form of the verb する (to do)]

- だめ no good; cannot; must not

- たくさん many; a lot

- どっち　でも　いい it's good either way; don't really care

- 家^{いえ} house; residence; dwelling

- 山^{やま} mountain

ANSWERS:

1) B – You can bring money. Just don't lose it.

2) B – The trip is to the ocean.

WEATHER FORECAST

つぎの ぶんを よんで、 しつもんに こたえて ください。

天気 よほう

おはよう ございます。今日 の 天気 です。

あさ	ゆうがた	よる

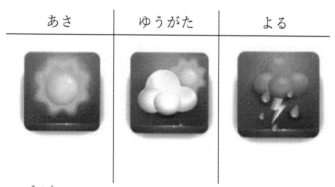

今日は、あさは はれる でしょう。

ゆうがたは、くもり でしょう。

今日は、２０ど まで あがる でしょう。よるは、９時 から 雨 が ふり はじめる ので、よる おそく かえる 人は、かさを もって 出かけて ください。

92

① 今日 の 天気は、どう ですか？

　A、ゆき

　B、はれ そして 雨

　C、くもり

　D、くもり そして ゆき

② よる おそく なる 人は、なにを もって いった ほう が いい ですか？

　A、カバン

　B、長ぐつ

　C かさ

　D、けいたいでんわ

GRAMMAR NOTES:

■ You often hear でしょう during forecasts to show likely weather.

> あさ　から　雨が　ふる　でしょう。 Rain should start from the morning.

> 今日は　はれ　でしょう。 Today will be sunny.

KEY VOCABULARY:

- 天気 weather [天 (heaven; sky) + 気 (spirit; nature; energy)]

- よほう forecast; prediction [kanji: 予報]

- おはよう　ございます good morning

- 今日 today [literally, "now day"]

- 今日の天気 today's weather [の (possessive marker)]

- あさ morning [kanji: 朝]

- はれる to be sunny [kanji: 晴れる]

- でしょう it seems; I guess

- ２０ど twenty degree [kanji: 度]

- まで up to; until

- あがる to rise; to go up [kanji: 上^あがる]

- よる evening; night [夜^{よる}]

- 9時^{くじ} nine o'clock

- から from

- 雨^{あめ} rain

- ふり　はじめる starts to fall [from 降^ふる (to fall); V-ます form + 始^{はじ}める is used when things start to happen or you start to do something]

- ので therefore; because of that

- よる　おそく late at night [kanji: 夜遅^{よるおそ}く; 夜 (night; evening) + 遅く (late)]

- かえる　人 a person who returns (home) [kanji: 帰^{かえ}る人^{ひと}; 帰る (to return; to come home) + 人 (person)]

- かさ umbrella [kanji: 傘^{かさ}]

- もって 出^でかけて ください please leave with an umbrella [from 持^もつ (to carry) + 出^でかける (to leave home; to go out)]

- 雪^{ゆき} snow

- くもり cloudy [kanji: 曇^{くも}り]

- カバン bag

- 長^{なが}ぐつ long boots; high boots [kanji: 長靴^{ながぐつ}; 長 (long) + 靴 (shoes; boots)]

ANSWERS:

1) B – Starts sunny but ends with rain.
2) C – Since it will rain, bring an umbrella

Please go to this website to download the MP3s for all the Japanese: (There is an exclusive free gift on kanji waiting there too)

http://japanesereaders.com/10n5r

As an extra added bonus, here is a coupon **for 10%** off your next order at www.TheJapanShop.com. Just use the coupon:

MATANE

(Just use the above word in CAPITALS; no minimum order amount!)

Thank you for purchasing and reading this book! To contact the authors, please email them at help@thejapanshop.com. See also the wide selection of materials for learning Japanese at www.TheJapanShop.com and the free site for learning Japanese at www.thejapanesepage.com.

Made in the USA
Columbia, SC
14 August 2024